A Journey to Self and Love

VOYAGER

A Journey to Self and Love

VOYAGER

A Journey to Self and Love

Khurram Shahzad

First Edition: 2019

Published by

Sanjh

46/2 Mozang Road, Lahore, Pakistan
Phone: 042-3735-5323. Cell: 0331-4686276
Email: sanjhpk@yahoo.com / sanjhpks@gmail.com

Dedication

*To Hira, who returned me more than I had desired,
and who is going to bother me for the rest of my life.*

Contents

Darks and Dreams(Part 1)

A Tale of Love(Part 2)

Shahzad's poetry emanates from the heart that is pure and it transposes the reader to Mir Sahib's valley-- the journey that remained missing from the poetry of Pakistani English poets. His bouts with absurdity, encounters with existential crises, skirmishes with nothingness and then his seeking refuge into the beloved's eyes fascinate and haunt the readers. The flight of imagination that is powerful and spontaneous takes us with it into the world that is simultaneously mesmerizing and jolting. The metrical setting doesn't upset the flow of thoughts and words which is his unique forte. His less western and more oriental poetry is intuitively sublime, philosophically complex and it inspires soul-searching. It invokes the lost oriental romantic feelings which have been averse to sheer materialism and redemptive force for Eastern spiritualism. His poetry revives the lost connection with what is galvanizing and aesthetically nirvanic in creation. In the materialistic and dead age, his poetry lights a ray of hope into the hearts blinded by the darkness of hedonism, selfishness and malignancy. The poetry lovers are sure to relish the bewitching journey with the voyager.

Mubashar Nawaz

Shahzad is a new voyager stranded positively beyond unseen horizons where his "titanic walls of intellect" and imagination do not make him "fall to the ground" but fly high to the open sky of an Aquarian creative frenzy. Beauty of his poetry is that without marginalizing monologic presence, it provides a dialogic silhouette and gives way to polysemic turn-taking. Like a talented camera man he knows how to freeze and melt a frame and then edit it accordingly between deep and shallow focuses. Poem by poem Shahzad denounces isolated paradox and develops situational vignettes through succinct but forceful lines which in future can brick a house of his own.

Jahanzabe Dhilon

Khurram Shahzad has been an acquaintance to me since 2009. His purity, his romantic ideas, his passion for humanism and his genuine expression are cult of his personality. It is natural that his poetry is a real mirror to his personality. I find, in his poetry, a Byronic hero who is passionate to excel in love, but purely in his own way. Indecisiveness, hanging between hope and despondency are some of the themes, and striving for reconciliation between physical and spiritual being is the main effort of Khurram Shahzad. A touch of Gothic setting, in some of his poems, is worth appreciating. Moreover, peculiar use of adjectives, Keatsian treatment to nature, sensuous imagery, dream-like atmosphere, and the amalgamation of ideal imagination and reality make his poetry unique, sublime and thought provoking. For me, the staunch and heart rendering feature of his poetry is the peculiar rhythm and lyricism. He has dealt with diverse experiences ranging from bequeathed love, uncertainty, complaints against beloved, negation of his being, to the most philosophical questions of life. His poetry enthralls the youth, elates the lover, consoles the rejected lover, inspires the passionate, and provides tranquility and reconciliation for the middle age. His first attempt is wonderful in style, genuine and bold in expression and pure in thought. In short, his poetry is lived, not written.

Junaid Mehmood

Blank

Darks and Dreams

Blank

A Voyager

A voyager stranded
In the open sky
Where terrible lightening
Laughter of clouds
Storms and heavy rains
Make him so terrified
That his intellect,
Though struggling to climb
The titanic walls of fear,
Badly fall to the ground
And gradually......
Die

My Ghost

An invisible tramp
Did never ramp
All I knew was his voice
That always seemed very nice
I questioned him
He counseled me
I notioned him
He excelled me
He argued well
For my friend and foe
He followed me
Wherever I'd go
My day and nights
With him did pass
I never noticed
My gain and loss

My life was stuck
How hard was luck!

I struggled for gain
But lost again
I never knew what I lacked
My head was stuffed my 'self' sacked
Once I impeached
My 'self' and preached
Of newer goal
Of refreshing soul
Then I saw a figure dark
That motioned me to an ark
We boarded on that ark to flee
To the depths of a dark-blue sea
We soon reached an island black
He left me and tapped my back
Wandering there, I did find
A tree and a hut blind
There wasn't any door to knock
I then cried that did rock
I heard a familiar voice
That once seemed quite sweet and nice
"You should go, you should go
Your 'self' has led you to a foe"
But I asked him to himself show
For the voice I heard, I did know
Then a figure appeared
He was in fear
"Though I'm your foe I'm your host"
When I turned to him, he was my ghost.

Life's Paradox

It seems as if
My life has shrunk
To a cellar
Dark and mysterious
Where I shriek and cry
My words are dry
As if meaningless

I pine for love
For life, for peace
But--
Miscommunicate
For the real
Doesn't exist
Or is very hard
To be believed
And the unreal
--- is equally vague.

"Nothing to be done?"
Is it true?
Even Done is nothing
Why to do!
"This is absurd"
Is this absurd?

The Inner Cry

A naked man
On scorching sand
Looks around
It's a far stretched desert.
His yelling then
Is the inner cry
Of a lost person.

From Wait to Hope

The dark black night
Seems to me
A pile of snakes
Minutes make a tiny one
And hours make a bigger
They sting by their turn
Keep stinging
It is painful
Or ticklish?
I know not
But it's disgusting
I'm waiting
For The Sun
That may burn them.
Burn them all!

An Oasis

A glass separates
Two worlds:
A bare desert
And an oasis.
A desert man
With stagnant eyes
And injured feet
Stares and craves
For he has tried
Thousand times
To break the glass
But defeated he sits
And watches the show.

My House

A vacant house
Where no one lives
No one takes, No one gives
Where no one comes and no one goes
Of this haunted house no one knows
Where voices of mine roar and roar
Staggering the walls, fall on floor
Where loneliness doth sting me hard
Where shrieks and cries grow and
retard
Where birds of flight have fears of
death
Where loves, relations do have dearth
This is my house; I do own
It will sink, when I may drown

Face of Truth

He was sitting
Near a lake
His eyes were cold
His lips did hold
His tongue;
He was silent
For ages
Dreaded and disheveled,
He was gazing
Upon the water,
Still and clear
As if it were a nymph
Or a fairy-beloved.
Meanwhile,
He did see
A visage bleak
Stared at it for long
And found it his own
Horrific!! Horrific!! "
He shrieked and said
"Clarity leads you to the truth"
He then left the wait waiting
As he knew the fate's fating.

Indecisiveness

I wander
As I've wanderlust
I saw a like-me
In a jungle
Wandering and searching
For his hunger
His eyes were sharp
His strength unyielding
His aim was perfect

He was carrying a bow
Of rare metal
Along with some
Poisonous arrows.
I kept watching his moves.
He sat by the trunk
Of the largest tree
Waiting for a prey.

A deer came
He aimed
But he, for a moment,
Stopped and watched
Her beauty and innocence
A lion leaped
And took her away
He waited again
This time it was a rabbit
He drew his bow
Aimed at it
But couldn't shoot
A hound came
Took it away
His hunger got severe
He decided to shoot
Whatsoever would come
A partridge sat on bunch
He aimed but the voice
Stopped him
A hawk took his prey again
There prevailed darkness
He had to go hungry
He had to go hungry.

Desires

Throwing my desires
In a furnace
I moved forward
Empty and desire less
Pity it is!
Life with desires
Leads to distress
And
Life without desires
Leads to disasters
Is there a third way??

Injustice

I wish to see the fragile
Of either the Aphrodites,
Or the Cupids,
Or the blind prophets of earthly love
If there's any
For I want to say,
"Why don't you fuck of
If you can't be just"?

A Blinking Thought

A blinking thought emerged,
Like a fresh morning rose.
I kept thinking before the night was closed.
The thought was a spy and it did try
To check my conscience and passions that lie,
Dull and drastic, dead and dry.
It inspired the dead passions producing a cry.
My heart supported to have a try
Now I am ready to take the plunge
Neither am I guilty nor discouraged
It is not scorn nor a scourge
But a blinking thought
That may blossom a flower as a whole,
To satisfy my restless soul.

Winter

A bird, left alone
In the summer of his life
Was sitting on a naked autumn tree
Waiting....
Hoping....
Forgetting the fact
That he had yet to survive winter.

Night's Silence

The time of night
On Lunar 15th
The full ripe moon after twelve
Gradually raised
The goon-clouds surrounded her
And veiled her with their blackness.
The utter darkness---
The howling of the jackals---
The roaring of tigers---
The groaning of the old---
The uneasiness of birds---
The eying of the owls---
And the whispering of the wind---
Altogether,
Choked the Night's silence
Lying on my cot,
I heard and saw
Silence disturbing life
Life disturbing silence.

A Passenger

He sits
With luggage under his arm
And waits for his train
A train reaches
But not his
He lights a cigarette
Waits again.
Another comes
But not his
He lights another cigarette
Waits again
He keeps seeing people
Boarding on and off
Those who get the train
Are happy
Those who board off
Are pale
He takes his luggage
Leaves the platform.

Confessions

You are the Greatest
You are the Merciful
I'm but an ungrateful human
Who hath pride
By his side
Who is valueless
In world's mess
Who craves and yearns
With desires burns
Who cleverly doth forgiveness seek
Facing you becomes a meek
Whose heart is grave
Where he doth bury
Cunningness, hypocrisy
And his fury

You do know well
Please do this must
Forgive the hearts
Stained with rust
For you made us
You know we're weak
Fall a prey
Then forgiveness seek

I am the one
Of those human beings
Who will be tempted
To their seeing
Forgive me God
For I'm in pain
Battered by desires
I'm sanely insane
I torture myself
With my own deeds
Give me shelter
Please, pay some heeds
Make me the one
Of the dear to you
I'll try my best
Just give me a clue...

Phantoms

In my childhood
A recurrent dream
Had haunted my mind
A phantom after me
And a dark well
In youth,
I feel the dark well
But not a phantom chasing me....
They are many...

A Ghost of Darkness

Standing against the well-wall
I looked down
And found
Shallow water and
A ghost in darkness
Hello!!!
I called him once
He returned me thrice.

Child of Night

I romanced the night
For hours' two
Kissed the darkness
Brushed the moon
Shook the stars
Satiated soon
She did conceive
My child then
Delivered on page
I don't know when

She did go, when Day arrived
The child with me has survived
I will keep her safe in book
She does have her mother's look

Consolation

The sky was blank
Without moon
Without stars

I hung a moon
And a few stars
For consolation.

What Ifs

What if the moon had
Turned herself upside down
Like a bucket
And poured her glow
Into chaos?
What if the stars
had Shed themselves down
Into abyss?
What if the Sun
Had fallen in love with earth
And drew her for a kiss?
Nothing such ever happened
Fear is Chaos! Fear is chaos!

An Outlander

A dark shady tree
A cart, worn out of shape
An extinguished 'huqa'
A dove sitting alone, was cooing
I with my red eyes saw and said
"Who lived here?

A Butterfly and a Boy

A butterfly with colored wings
Flatters the flowers in early springs
The flowers blush and swing with breeze
Welcome her with smiles and squeeze
She brushes the cheeks crimson red
Lurks and flies on white lily's head
Soothes them with some kisses cool
Enchants them and their loves rule
Spring ends and flowers wither
It steals nectar and moves farther
Finds new beds if flowers in bloom
Forgetting those it left in gloom
Soon it is meshed in a Boy 's hand
Who tip-toe comes leaving a band

A Desert Man

A vast desert
A dark black horse
He sprints vaguely
Forces his limbs
He runs, does run
Showing his wrath
Scratches the sand
For he's no path
There's scorching heat
He burns his feet
He sits for whiles
After some miles
He shrieks, does din
For its his skin
That melts and burns

It's now he learns
About the nature
Of the desert
There's sand no track
He lifts his back,
Musters his strength
Runs straight at length
For hundred-mile
In a great guile
He reaches a Pass
There's bulk of grass
Inside of it
The land is cool
The birds do chirp
Their songs do rule
He rests, he eats
He himself treats
His self , his soul
With all blessings
In shades he sits
His mind, he quits
But....
Something in him
Does prick his hards
His soul can't stop
His mind retards
Leaving all this
Where does he go?
I am quite aware
Do you know?

Vertigo

Heights are hard I love going high
Had I wings, I would love to fly
I climb the walls and choose not door
My struggling steps do take me shore
Climbers often a song do sing
"The slippery walls are hard to cling"
Afraid to be a stone, I don't take long
For me, it's just a mermaid's song
Heights enchant even falls have a taste
Falling down would not be a waste
I do know why I climb the walls
I love not height but desire fall

Dreams

Dreams are trumpets
That summon us
To a world
Unknown
And
We submit
For quite a time
If we dream good
And if otherwise,
We spring up.

This life
Is a Dream
Of the Real
Springing up
Or submitting
Depends upon the Dream

Instinct vs Desire

Instincts guide, desires derail
Loving someone and being loved
Is a clash of instinct and desire
That disturbs the anatomy of love
The lover, desirous of being loved,
Eclipses his instinct—
— the prima
When it comes to love
He is fucked up!

A Scar on Darkness

In deep, dense, dark
He could see nothing
For the darkness
Had utterly prevailed
There was uniformity....
Even his internal darkness
Became one with the external
He enjoyed the beauty
Of the dark
Where he was invisible
Then the moon appeared
And he said,
"Moon is but a scar on darkness's face"

Moons

She, lonely and deserted,
Was standing,
Being amazed
At darkness
Turning redness
And blueness
Tuning pale,
She did see moons,
Four full and a half
Of different sizes
Of different colors.
Looking up, she asked
"Is this how one lives?"
A voice replied
"This is how one's supposed to live"

My Visage

With my hypocrisy
and sins
How can I be stiff?
I'm hypocrite or sinful
or both, I know not
But I have fears
That I am.
I may not be
For the others
May be my comrades
This is self-consolation
Or an assumed truth
I know not either
But....
I know one thing
I never wish to be a hypocrite.

A Hawk in Me

He is fierce not mild
He is extremely wild
He urges me to prey
The birds, white, golden, grey
He is a royal king
Wishes for a rare thing
Gets it in a mare flight
For his flights do have might
He is inspiration
Shows me destination
I am idle, he is fit
He does fly, when I sit
He is the best of me
He weeps not like a 'she'
I'm coward, he is strong
I take time , he not long

Insects' Nature

When the flowers bloom in spring
The insects on colors cling
On the flowers, are they fed--
The delicate petals red
They suck the nectar with lust
And crave the time when they bust
The red, the weak, and fragile
Taint the bed and sacred soil
That's bitter, what else be done?
Nature offers shows for fun

Exhaustion

I mirrored my visage
It's pale, and withered
Shattered and tired
For the age is creeping
Gently rapid
But there had been something---
That kept me young
Alas! It had been.

Eternity

Behold my dear, Behold!
The Night embroidered
With silvery material
Glows and Twinkles
Without wrinkles
It's smooth and calm
With hot-cold nip--
No flip, no zip
Then gradually.....
It shrouds the naked
Body of the tired Day
And
Lasts forever.

Cost of Memories

I set some earthen lamps
On the shelves
Made twigs of memories
And my blood their oil
That feeds them,
Burns for them
And lights them...
The memories are alive
At the cost of my blood
They would die
When I cease to be...

"You" & "I"

"I" is a plague
"You" is love
But...
We have "I"
"You" we lack
We will die
And be dark
Without love....
Think about "you".

Stubbornness

The wet sand on the shore
Feels good to walk on.
The waves lick my feet;
Beg me to return
But I have to wade in--
To have a row with The Sea
.......A lot to explore

A Whisper of Past

Our past like a ghost
Tip-toes us
And ....
At present
Whispers into our happiness
That is always
Weak and fragile
Submissively docile
It swells in rage
Bursts in winks
Turns its page
To end methinks....

Another Moon

The queen moon
With a glow-crown
Was sitting
Among the stars
Being flattered
About her beauty and charm
That something
Dazzled her glow
For a moment.
Then she saw
A Cooler glow
Bigger in size
Brighter in color
Another moon....
That passed near
Eclipsing her charms...
Now she veils
Now she veils.

A Glass of Water

Among
A bottle of wine
A glass of water
And
An empty glass
......
I'm the glass of water.

A 'Have to Live'

Nights are dark
So is light
Love is hard
So is life
Darkness, light
Love and life
Are indispensable--
We have to undergo
And------ live.

A Cuckoo's Coo

I dreamt of being stranded
In a groove
Finding a way.
A cuckoo's coo
Made me struggle
To get away.
I got rid of that groove
And went after
That frequent coo
Since then,
I've been finding
The cuckoo
For it has been cooing
In my dream
In my real

Unyielding Spirit

Sometimes man,
Stranded among
The ferocious wind--
The roaring of the clouds--
The vehement lightening--
And furious rain,
Struggles hard
To get away
Utilizing his utmost capacity
His sagacity, his talent
But nature's ferocity
Sweeps him cleanly
He gets defeated
But the defeat
Can't pacify
The dispositions
Of aggression that
Electrify him.
He musters up
Courage to go again.

Identification

I, with the moon and sea-shore,
Spent a lot of time
The seas encountered
Not once but many times
His friskiness met
My undaunted spirit
His rage submitted to mine
The night-queen whispered
Glowing within darkness
Causing the waves
Of his and mine to rise
And submerge into each other
We became one—
The night passed and the sun rose
All is forgotten, all is forgotten.

I'm 'Two'

I am two;
A dream and a real
The real is coward;
For he has fears
The dream is power;
For he goes near
To you,
Creating another 'you'

Both do love
Both do care
For each other's groans
'For each other's fear
But...
The dream is bubble
The real is real.

Innocence

Two boys, fighting
For a piece of bread,
Smashed and boxed
Each other hard.
Finally,
One succeeded
In snatching the piece.
Drenched in mud,
He ran and sat
On a rock.
When he was about to eat
He looked at the other one
Went to him, smiled
And gave him half of it.

A New Year

When past is misty
And life unclear
What new year?

When present sucks
And future is fear
What new year?

When the beloved disdain
And friends do Jeer
What new year?

These may be logics
Of many of peers
For New year

The reality is harsh
Quite bitter and Sheer
But let's cheer
For New Year

The brave don't face
Reality with fear
So let's cheer
For New Year

We know well Past
And Future's unclear
Let's cheer
For present my dear
And New year.

Triumph

A bare ground, a lonely man
Standing against the fierce wind
That forces hard to lift his feet
By fluttering his hair
Pinning his body
And blinding his eyes.
Though his feet shiver,
His body quiver
He stands, he does stand
The Wind slows down
And turns its path
He opens his arms
And screams loudly
Exhaling pain,
Announces his triumph.

The Gardner

Passing a Garden
I hold my bosom and behold
Oranges ,mangoes,
Rasp berries, and strawberries
Dripping with juice
My mouth waters ,
My thirst gets severe
I jump and jump to hold and tear
But . . . . .
Before I reach
The Gardener does appear
I go thirsty
With the thirst sheer.

Humans!!

Sometimes trees
Bearing fruit
Want the fruit
To be picked;
For they are prepared
And ripened.
The land
That grows tree
Like a mother
Waits to taste the fruit
When no one picks,
The tree's shaking
Land's lust
And fruit's own exhaustion
Make it fall into dust
The fruit is wasted away
So are humans!!

To a Sister

What grieves more when a sister doth
ignore
Her preferences, herself, and her life's lore
She craves for nothing but her brother's
life
She knocks and knocks, O God, your door

Her brother's a flower, a darling thing
To whom did Cancer, the monster, cling
She spent her days and her nights with him
But could not shun off that monstrous thing

This swelled her heart and her eyes bled
For him, she smiled like a flower red
She offered her stem cell, her heart, her blood
But docs couldn't reverse what had been said

Though, he was taking in the darkness
dips
The boy-flower still had a smile on lips

A Voice

A fear jeers at me
"Your being is decaying
Your restless soul callous
Cloudy, blinded by trash
Your fire is turning to ash
Your purpose is about to drawn
Your heart with tick grass overgrown"
The jeering of fear inspires a voice
Which reminds me of bare choice
"Your being 's plant has turn to tree
Avoid illusions to set you free
Remember the time when it bore
Strong and stalwart branches four
Love, faith, intellect, and devotion
They will keep you in a motion
The tree one day will bend down
Strong branches may bring you crown
You may see or not see
Fruit hanging on your tree"
The voice has thought me to dare
I am not afraid of fear's sneer.

A Fierce Wind

I stand still and motionless
In the calm sea
Within me
A fierce wind
Loaded with sins
Rushes
Creating a storm
In the calm sea
I stumble on the tumultuous waves
Fall and crawl
But.....
I am swept across.

The Lamp

*You lit a lamp
In the dark room
Where....
Life would stagger
If moved
Where desires would die
Of suffocation
Now...
Keep feeding the lamp.*

Bright Night

When the moon ornaments
Night's gloomy face
And the stars gather
One by one
To add to the beauty
Of the bride
Lying in my couch,
I enjoy the melancholy
It incites within me
But abhor
The envy I feel
For the night—
— she is ornamented
And I'm dark.

To Dream is Human

They have shattered visages
They have barren eyes
They have frozen feet
They have inner cries
They have choked voices
They have cold sighs
They have begging-hands
They have tired tries
Yet......
To dream is human!

Dream-Dome

Snuffing out candle-flame,
I had a ride on sleep-horse
Reached a dream-dome
And saw
Many dreamers
With their dream-boxes
Begging for the fulfillment
Of their dreams.
They opened their boxes
And I did too
But...
I had to return;
For I lost my dreams
In such a crowd.
Finding them
Was a life-long task.
I left them there
I left them there.

A Tale of Love

Balnk

Loves

For every love I acted well
I promised love and said I shall
I gave them only one of Me
To their visions, I let them see
Some of Me were harsh, some cool
Some others acted like a fool
No one can claim to have me all
I have never seen such a fall
I always kept my 'self' in spare
None could destroy, none could dare
Now I'm afraid, for you have seen
All my sides red, white and green
Losing you, I would lose
Me... my poetry... and my muse

My Love for You

My love for you
Is not foolish
To claim stars and moon
Not irrational
To inhale seas
Not selfless
To sacrifice you or itself
Not hyperbolic
To cater all happiness
But...
It is pure
Like the honey in hive
Caring like a mother
Wild like a beast out of food
Innocent like an infant
Proud like a hawk
Cute like a dove
Selfish like a human
And...
Subtle like death
Can you digest?

Surrender

Had I a pen to write my fate
I would have written thee my mate

Had I a life to live till doom
I would have loved and shun thy gloom

Had I a heart with space of Sea
I would have given all to thee

Had I a mind to think like gods
I would have composed you all plods

But I'm human, a fragile being
I've to surrender to my seeing

A Desert Girl

Don't be lonely
O desert girl!!
The Sun's at peak
The scorching heat
You may burn
Your feet, your face
Have some shade
And a tree your friend
O!! I am foolish
You are a desert girl.

I often Think of Death and Doom

I often think of death and doom
They live with me, with me they groom
Death holds my mind, bruises my heart
I think of you, and life and art

What life is this that has a death?
Tomorrow, we may not have breath
I do know well that this is true
Death be harsh if I won't have you

What if I die when I don't live?
Without you love, my life I give
My art be a waste, my life dark
Death may take me without a mark

I want your love that's life, my art
Come, let me live and be my part

An Image

A look of anger or a look of
indifference?
Curiosity sheds from her eyes
Her cheeks take shape
To smile or grin?
Confusion prevails!
I shall wait upon her
For I surmise
Her lips that have
Sucked forth
Hue and dew
From flowers
May spread to smile
When she shifts
Her eyes from the sun
To the moon
Or may grin
At the sun
For his insolence...

Now and Then

I was a rational fool,
A stupefied fellow
With grave thoughts
And some rules
You.... came
Elevated me
Inspired me
And.....
I left my rules
Now I am
No more rational
But just a fool.

A Flower Girl

Meticulously did she bind
Flowers of various kind
Pink, white, red and gold
With petals of many folds
She threw them up and let them fly
And then she did see up in sky
The bliss I then saw on her face
Like free and charming beauty-dace
When the flowers down did fall
Her smile and smell had they all
She did vanish after the show
Collecting flowers, I thought how?
The moment shines in mind like pearl
I won't forget that flower girl

Vorfreude

Tired and exhausted
Frozen and frosted
From the real of reality
From the world of cruelty,
They feel not say
How anxious are they!
To have it done
Leave fret and fun
Of the world that is harsh
And the people those're rash
They decide to fly
Above and high
To discover in space

A peaceful place
Where they would've hopes
No world, no 'nopes'
Here they fly!!
With the mind's eye
Quite far they go
No one would know
Kissing the cloud
With shrieks loud
They move and move
To themselves prove
The each other's love
In the space above
The space is cool
Nobody's to fool
But just the peace
And serenity
They stop for a while
In a magical guile
Look each other's face
For they know no pace
There moves are slow
But they race to flow
Their love through eyes
Without I's and My's
Their eyes flow
With tears glow
For love or triumph
I do not know
She motions to walk
For they cannot talk
He smiles and moves
To avoid the groove.
His hand she holds
His fears she folds
They walk with breeze
With love and ease

In their suits in boots
Knowing nothing of routes.
Fortunately, soon
They come by the moon
She looks at her
Her eyes doth blur
With tears of happiness.
He questions her fate
The silver plate
That borrows light
From the sun bright
Though she glows
Romances flows
She is alone
The space-born
"Alone" reminds him
Of his earthly fur
She holds his hand
And points at her
"Look at her for she is young
 Let's sing for her, songs un-sung"
He smiles and says
As around were fays
"I sing to moon
But moon is 'you'
You ask me sing
My moon, I do"
She giggles and blushes
Her face doth flashes
She asks him stay
For one whole day

An Impression

When you look at yourself
Steal my eyes
For a moment,
You will fall in love
With what you see

A Walk in the Fog

Your love for winter drove me to
A landscape, fog and lovely you
Your hands on cheeks and eyes on tops
Of green hills where fog flies and hops
She crept, coiled and fluttered her fur
You held my hand and walked to her
She brushed your cheeks, your lips, your
eyes
I envied her and held my sighs
Your cheeks were moist your lips too
I clutched your hand, what else I'd do
I held your face, there ran a bead
My heart did throb, my eyes bleed
Your shivering lips, teary eyes
I braced my breadth, and slurped my cries
Your visage slipped and sand did run
Through my fingers in desert-sun.

The Busy Moon

O busy moon! Look at us!
When we sit in your glow
You ignite a feeling
Of love mysterious;
Our eyes romance bodies
Our hearts pump and clutch breaths

But you're busy with many;
Look at each and every love
I suggest you to look at us
You can't deal with everyone
Though you stir the deep passion
You can't execute romance

Contract yourself, encircle us
At least we love well in your glow
To make you see us in the flow

The Feel

When the heart beats irregularly
And the breath takes intervals,
When the body loses force
And mind submits to imagination,
When I have all and nothing
And that nothing I enjoy
When melancholy becomes happiness
And happiness melancholy
When heart becomes clouds
And rains through eyes,
I feel, I feel for you

A "you".

I've spent or wasted
My life...
I've been lavish
Or thrifty
I've been strong
Or drifty?
I know not.
But ...
I haven't lived
For I don't have--
A "you".

A Brief Encounter

A lad I saw
Very tough very raw
Whole life did he bear
For love was his fear
He wasn't hostile
But rough like soil
His life had hards
A house of cards
He played every move
To learn to prove
His strength his might
His head his right

But life is life
One has to strife
He paid his debt
His fear he met
A lass very fair
Riding white mare
She waved a fur
He fell for her
His eyes did meet
Her eyes did cheat
The crowd of men
And met his then
Another man
With a hand fan
Received her well
With smile, with bell

She went with him
But left her eyes
In man who stood
In grief, with sighs

And She--
Though lives with him,
Thinks of the glance
That was quite brief
That was a half-chance

Why She Smiled?

I met her
She was strange
With hair disheveled
And eyes.... barren
Her face turned pale
Her heart turned lead
Her hands didn't shake
For she hadn't herself fed
With happiness.
She sat by the shore
I did then implore
She did not move
Or did not try
Just watched the sea
With gestures dry
The sea was fierce
The waves made noise

He roared and roared
She stared, did poise
At last she smiled
And jumped into sea
Vanished in eye wink
I couldn't even plea
Now
I sit by the shore
And myself implore
Why she smiled
Why she smiled.

Your Smile

When you smile
My happiness widens
With the spreading of
Your lips.
I want this happiness
To prolong
Can you smile forever?

A Proposal

If I were the sun
And you be the moon
Our love would be distant
Yet unique and never ending
The sun is fierce
The moon is tender
He is large
She is slender
They do romance
Just see and sense
He does pour warmth

Even from a distance
She does receive
Without resistance
Notice their love
They are--
Adorable.
When she is not around
He is hot and bright
When she arrives,
He's cool at her sight
Soon he does go
So that she'd glow
In some part of world
Every day they meet
Distant is their love
Yet there's no cheat
Their life is love
They won't be apart
Love's been with them
From the very start.
Let's love like them
Let's get it done
Will you be my moon?
If I be your sun?

A Dialogue on Love

A lad and a lass like Laila and Qais
Dwelt with grace when against was a mass
They lent none ears, to none did they speak
They breathed like one and avoided the meek

Bullshit! You think I'm fool to ear such
crap
Such country of love doesn't exist on map
Breathing like one and loving for life
Ohh!! It is a myth and a mere strife

The narrative of love exists, did reign!
Your shallow disbelief will go in-vain
"Love's an ever fixed mark", did Master say
The lovers blossom like the month of May

Love is a trash, an illusion, a slash
It causes ambivalence and a clash
In minds of the young and the grown-ups too
Huh! it sucks them all and leaves not a clue

All losers do say that love is a trash
Because they lose and can't this blessing cash
Love is worship, a spirit and a truth
It soothes the soul and the body doth ruth

The mind is the boss for it does
command
The body has lust and it does demand
Where is the truth, the spirit and the soul
Love is lust of the body as a whole

Love and lust are the North and the
South
Logics should be apt, mind opening your mouth!
We don't lust when love, we don't love when
lust.
Lust needs body only, love finds spirit must
Alone cannot body love nor can spirit do
Love is the name of the mixture of the two

I don't agree, though arguments I lack
Love is foolish, an idealistic sound track

Not only arguments but words you lack
Love is healing sunshine while lust is black

A Memory

You look at the moon
It shrinks into your eyes
Don't blink
Let me see the moon.

Craving

I held her hand and drew her near
She was nervous, drenched in fear
I wore her fingers in my hand
All turned in fairy piece of land
I wrapped my arm around her waist
She stood still awed, I made no haste
I gazed at her to meet her gaze
Her eye-balls moved like were in daze
I felt her, smelt her sensed her too
Repressing her smile, she stared in lieu
I held quite near my lips and head
But I found 'nothing' in her stead
A dream she is, I thought it grave
She is here and for her I crave

Murdered by a Shadow

He sat near a throw
A trumpet did blow
She came downstairs
With flakes, with snow
His heart did throb
When he lifted his brow
She was a magic
That affects quite slow
He gazed and gazed
For he was so amazed
By her beauty, charm
And the words she phrased
"I'm love, I am fire
Don't follow you desire"
He wanted that love and fire

That was only his desire
She took him to her land
Where mixed were snow and sand
Where moons and star she owned
That would come down if she frowned
Winds and clouds were her friends
She would play them to the ends

Fascinated, and enchanted
He told her that he was haunted
She said nothing and did go
And returned with sand and snow
"I dwell with Paradoxes,
Many a Pandora boxes
Sand and snow when do meet
Snow doth melt, or sand doth eat
I do love you; for I did wait
Leave now, don't serve as bait"
He did leave the place and her
Now he sits, with memory blur,
With her thoughts, in the meadow
He was murdered by a Shadow

Oct 5, The Blood Moon

We loved the moon,
We romanced her
I pictured when
You stanced her

Her glow for us
Was a magic
Her flow for us
Was pelagic

She smiled for us
We gleed at night
She veiled in clouds
We hugged in white

But today....
She is blood
Our eyes flood!
Her rage is severe
We have to bear
The parting of Us
The Life-Long Fuss!

An Angelic Girl

An angelic girl
With white shells
Playing on the sea shore,
Observes the Sun beams
Piercing into the waves
Eyes into Sun's eye.
Spreading her lips
To half a smile,
She turns around
Leaving them behind.

Her Eyes

In the evening
She stood alone
Watching the setting sun
Getting down into the ocean
Ohh!! Her eyes
Filled with tears
Kept watching.
What I saw was amazing;
The sun sinking
Into the ocean
And....
Both sinking
Into her eyes.

The Fog

The fog now creeps
In silence doth speak
Some horrors so grave
Some myths that crave
To emerge and merge
In the present.
Nobody does know,
Nobody does hear
The mysteries of fog
And the fears severe.
Here she comes!!
A curious form
Longs to explore
The ancient norm
She doth implore
The fog thick
About the mysteries
And questions quick
She feels at home
With the fog white;
Touches, inhales
Feels its might
I am amazed;
For she doth enjoy
I couldn't implore it
When I was a boy.

A Girl I Know

A girl I know
With dreams bright
She talks about clouds
And the starry nights
She embraces rain
And enjoys sights.
Her dreams are vivid;
For she does paint
Some beeches, seas
And past that's faint
She romances the moon,

Feels the sun at noon
She loves young birds
Not wild and goons
She absorbs the pain
Doth nothing gain;
A bleak smile
And a self-complain
Her dreams shatter
She cannot cater
A sense of joy
A sense of joy.

A fall in Love

Though words I say may not convince
For days are hard and heart doth wince
Yet I do write for I did earn
Your heart, with words, that I did yearn

My words were strong, my heart intense
So was my feel, so was my sense
With one mistake I did lose all
The forbidden fruit caused my fall

Now all is same but said unsaid
The waxing words have turned to lead
I feel my heart and feed them blood
My anxious soul and my eyes' flood

Your feel and sense are tools for me
If they do work, my words will be
Soften your heart, un-cage my soul
My words may work for greater goal

My Poetry

Every night ....
I love composing a good line
For creative pleasure
My eyes roll and stagger with your apparition
And the line that carries `you'
Is the better, and is true.

My Imagination

When I imagine her, my reason goes to
dogs
My brain ceases to think,
My heart feasts at her sight
Overjoyed, it throbs as if dancing
With her moves
It accepts no philosophy my mind pours
forth
But the philosophy of love
That seems ridiculous to modern minds
Is the deeper, the sweeter and the
softer

Which enchants and lulls
Taking me to forgetfulness;
A better place---
Where I know no fears---
Where reason's complexity fades--
Where I feel relaxed in her company.
When she smiles,
Her eyes twinkle
Her face glows.
When she speaks,
I forget there be any singing bird on
earth
When she looks at me,
I feel like living.
I want to be in this state
O reality!! Don't haunt me
I don't know you
I don't know you.

Would That!! .1

If I were a butterfly,
You would run after me
Catch me, and smile.

If I were a dream,
You would see me
Imagine me, and paint

If I were rain,
You would feel me
Touch me, and splash
If I were a moon
You would wait for me
Point to me, and glow

If I were a good moment
You would live me
Enjoy and be happy

Would that I were,
But I am the one
You are immune to.

A Tale of Woe

She told him go
And bade him bye
Her face was harsh
And her eyes dry
Her frowns I know
But know not heart
Her lips were cold
When she did part
He stood in shock
But did not cry
His heart did bounce
He did not sigh
His face was blank
Eyes didn't have feel
He knew or not
But it was real
He was hollow
An empty base
I could not help
Taking his case

I know that once
In each other's arms
They spent nights
That were their balms
Her eyes he adored
And loved her hair
Her cheek he pulled
But kiss...didn't dare
Her smile was life
He lived it well
I'm quite shocked
How would he dell?

It's end of love
Or here begins?
She went, he's gone
Whose faults whose sins?
"The more you love
The more it hurts"
"The one who loves
Doth always flirt"
Sagacious sayings
But what is truth?
When they did part
My heart did clueth
Neither of them
Was fake or flirt
To save each other
They had to hurt.

You're

You're an inspiration;
You're my imagination
Leave me not
Among the hounds
Reality lets upon us---
Among the noise
It pours upon us---
Among the frustrations
It feeds us with---
Among the hypocrites
Who smile at us---
Among the uncertainties
That batter us---
And in dismay
That crushes us

Take me away!!
Take me away
To the world you imagine
Where daisies smile
Where roses beguile
Where moon winks
Where heart thinks
Where twittering skylarks
Feed our ears
Where tigers feed
Some little deer
Where cuckoo sings
In enchanting voice
Where deserts overgrow
With grass green
Where streams in sun
Do brightly sheen
Where rivers-snakes
Do run a race
Where lovers win
With a special grace...

Let not the reality
Be cruel to you
You're a goddess
You never knew.

Me & You

My words need shape
My eyes need sight
I want a sweet touch
When the moon is bright

My ears do hear
The voice intense
The fragrance's sweet
I do now sense

Abstract is love
I crave for its form
It's fierce, it's wild
Come calm the storm

Your touch I miss
Long for a kiss,
Breathe me today
Take my soul away

My arms do feel
My heart does bounce
You're, are you not?
Your shape I pounce
Come sit with me
In the bright sun
Where fields are green
On which we'd run

You can do it
Or can't you do?
Let us be one
Or make me two;
......
One me-one you!

Us

A like-you and a like-me
Met at a dark blue sea
They ran, they played
We watched, we stayed
She smiled with glees
Hair touched her knees
He glared and felt
His heart did melt
A wave did raise
With rush, with blaze
We sat and saw
With love and awe
He went to her

With eyes quite blur
His sense was haste
He didn't want to waste
Then touched her hair
And neck that's bare
She tilted 'bit
A feeling lit
She could not stop
In arm did hop
He braced her tight
Feel was on height
His head he bent
To smell her scent
She moved and armed
Her soul she calmed
Let's hug like us
Leave all the fuss
We have the feel
Let's make it real.

A Moment

O rose-faced damsel!
Your lips, the dewy petals
Oh!! Don't wipe
Let me have a drop of eternity.

Metaphors

A girl in dismay
Thinks vaguely
Indecisively
Moves her hand
That is to pick
A stone of two;
A white and a black
I aspire
She should pick....
The white one.

An Aura

Lying in bed
The pained sense
Pains my present
And an aura
Makes it ecstatic.
The former is real
The latter's my want.
I stood still
Eying the Sun
That dazzled my eyes
But not my spirit.
With such eyes,
I see in to a cup of tea
And the aroma of tea
Along with your voice
Calling me smoothers my sense.
I still am stranded
Between pain and you.

Decision

After ten years
You may receive
A book
Of poetry or prose
Decide...
You need it
With only my sign
Or a "your love"?

A Moment to Relish

I stared upon her
For quite long
Her eyes dragged me
Her lips incited me
Her heart touched me
I took my lips upon hers
My lips shivered
My heart smiled
But I braced myself
For I think too precisely
"Live the moment "
I decided to undecided
"Life has death"
I thought
"Let's wait upon the beauty
Of the moment
It may live
But....
What if
I die without living it?

A Song to Love

Be my night and be my day
Hold me tight and let me say

My nights are long for I'm alone
I feel you in my skin and bone

My days are dull for I am done
With all the fury, fret and fun

At night I crave the cuddles soft
Thinking of you my mind does loft

At days I work, with thoughts of you
My focus spoils, what should I do?

My mornings are fresh when I dream
Of you with me in sky in stream
I can't suppress the passions grave
With them for you I crave and crave

A Blessing

Who else could inspire, when I'm
blessed
With a fairy-girl who fits me the best
Though she is away, my feel is strong
I drag her where she does belong
Here she smiles to stars and the moon
The night worms will now gather soon
Wait to see butterflies at night
With worms they make quite a sight
The worms do light their tail and glow
With butterflies to her they bow
She does glow in colorful light
Her hands move in bliss to height
In happiness when she points at them
Her face glitters like that of a gem
Looking at her, I smile and say
I do want her for life to stay

Good Morning

I slept with a feel
I woke with it
You're all with me
Not in a bit
Your scent is fresh
And skin like wool
Your breath is mint
I feel it cool
Your hair on face
Dazzle the dawn
You grow on me
Like sun at morn
You wear your arms
Around my neck
Like the mornings
With flowers deck
You move and hum
You smile and squeeze
Your touch on me
Is pleasant breeze

I won't get up
I lose the feel
Let's lie for life
Let's have a deal

Yearning for Love

Our bed is a haven where we two dwell
In the shade of love, we grow quite well
Your fragrance is spread in the folds of
sheets
I mop not this, my passions it heats
I remember the kisses that you fed
I do feel the touch, when lie in bed
Your delicious smell I sense I implore
When finds not you, my heart deplores
My arms do twist, and crunch, and
crave
Your body and skin, and love you gave
I wait for you, your spirit, and soul
I am in parts, come make me whole

Be Not Jealous

I suggest, be not jealous;
For its three eyed monster
Setting one eye for each
You, me, and anyone.

I like your being jealous
Of anyone for me
For it's out of your love.
But remember the eyes;
One enrages you to ashes,
One retards my image,
One destroys anyone.

Hit his eyes and kill at once.
With arrow of trust, you hit two
One for me, one for you.
Your being not jealous, hit the third
So be not jealous, and save us all.

How it Rains?

The naked clouds
Rubbing their skins
With each other,
Roar and laugh.
The moon bashfully smiles
And hides herself.
The sky wraps
The stars in black cloak
The sun for the moment
Grins and go.
Then it rains.
Now I got....
Why rain begets romance!